Life in Nelson's Navy

Contents

CHAPTER 1

Joining the Navy

For a young man with good connections and some education, the Royal Navy in the days of Nelson offered an exciting career. He would join the most successful armed force in the world, with the possible exception of the French army – a force which defeated every opponent who dared to put to sea, often against heavy odds. He could see the world, fight the enemies of his king, and possibly become rich through prize money. He might hope to follow in the tradition of Nelson himself, who was killed in 1805 after leading his fleet into three major victories.

Much depended on the young man's own talents: he could rise to become an admiral, and possibly a knight or a lord. His parents might worry about losing their son at sea, but for a large family a naval career had the great advantage that his education was almost free. It was no job for a quiet, studious boy, and he had to be as courageous as Jane Austen's brother Francis:

> Fearless of danger, braving pain,
> And threaten'd very oft in vain.

The boy would start at the age of about 12 or 13. His parents had to find a Royal Navy captain who was willing to take him on, perhaps a relative or a political or business connection. The young Horatio Nelson was lucky that his uncle, Captain Maurice Suckling, was appointed to a ship when the boy was just the right age. Arriving on board, the young man would be rated as a captain's servant or a volunteer first class. He was often bewildered at first. He lived in a mess below decks with the other boys, where anarchy often reigned. Above decks, there were perhaps 40 miles of rope rigging that he had to understand, and up to 100 guns. He might find himself in battle within days of joining, as did Frederick Hoffman in the frigate *Blonde* in the English Channel in 1793: 'Two of the enemy's frigates were now within gunshot and the two others nearing us fast. We had almost despaired of escaping, when fortunately one of our shot brought down the advanced frigate's fore topsail yard.'

The young man would carry on with his education under the ship's chaplain or schoolmaster, and learn navigation under the master. After three years he could be promoted to midshipman and begin to take some responsibility, perhaps taking charge of a group of seamen for welfare and disciplinary purposes, commanding one of the ship's boats or a group of guns in action, or acting as deputy to the officer of the watch. He might spend some time in the more senior post of master's mate. After a total of six years he was entitled to sit a stiff oral examination before three captains, which not everyone passed. William

Badcock was examined by Sir Andrew Snape Hammond in May 1805, and on the way in he met a midshipman who had failed. Badcock was questioned on 'double altitude, bearings and distances &c.' and asked to issue the orders to take an imaginary ship out of harbour. He passed, bowed to the officers and bolted out of the room to be 'surrounded in a moment by the other poor fellows, who were anxiously waiting their turn to be called in for examination'.

For every lieutenant on the average ship, there were about a hundred others – seamen, craftsmen, marines, servants, boys and unskilled landsmen. The seamen were the most important, the skilled men who steered the ship, handed the sails and took charge of the guns in action. The navy had no training scheme for them, and most of them were recruited from merchant ships, where they too had begun their careers as boys. According to the economist Adam Smith, their skill and dexterity are much superior to that of almost any artificers, and though their whole life is one continuous scene of danger and hardship, yet for all the skill, for all the hardships and dangers, while they remain in the condition of common sailors, they receive scarce any other recompense than the pleasure of exercising the one and of surmounting the other. Their wages are not greater than those of common labourers at the port which regulates the rate of seaman's wages.

Merchant wages were high in wartime, and the press gang was often necessary to get men into the navy. Popular myth suggests that this terrorised whole districts, and dragged unwilling landsmen into the fleet. In practice the members of the gang often lived in fear of their own safety, and they usually took only experienced men for the navy. Some gangs were based in seaport towns such as London, Liverpool, Hull and Newcastle. Others operated off the coast, stopping merchant ships and taking part of the crew off. Some gangs were members of the crews of warships at sea, some were based permanently on shore. It was a hard life for the officers and men of the gang, and in 1814 Lieutenant Forbes in Greenock wanted to be replaced 'in consequence of the repeated insults I meet with in the streets of Greenock, and the mob having proceeded even up the stairs to the door of my lodgings . . . It is hard to say what so ferocious a people might do.' At Hull early the next year, a seaman escaped the press gang by slipping out of his jacket. He was recaptured but,

> A number of workmen joined the mob and liberated the sailor. A regular chase, or running fight, was kept up through Low-gate. The gang applied in vain for assistance at the Mansion House, and dispersed to their several homes; but the mob, now exasperated, proceeded in a riotous manner through the market place and Humber Street to the press

gang's rendezvous . . . the mob (many of whom were sailors) completely wrecked the house.

Apart from low wages, sailors hated the navy because they could not leave at the end of a voyage. When their ship came out of service, they were usually transferred to another without any choice in the matter, and perhaps separated from their messmates and friends. Unless they were ill enough to be invalided out, or they deserted, they were in until the end of the war. When he was impressed in 1794, Seaman John Nicol wrote, 'I found myself in a situation I could not leave, a bondage which had been imposed on me against my will.' The French Revolutionary War lasted nine years, from 1793 to 1802, and the Napoleonic Wars from 1803 to 1815, with one short break. Men had no absolute right to shore leave, and captains were reluctant to grant it in case the men deserted. It was possible for a man to spend several years without setting foot on shore.

Arriving on board a warship, the experienced seamen were rated by the first lieutenant. Some might become petty officers, taking charge of a group of men working on one of the masts, or giving orders to the crew as boatswain's mates. The more experienced men would become able seamen, if they had at least seven years at sea and had various skills. Less experienced men were rated as ordinary seamen, and in 1807 they had a basic pay of £1 5*s* 6*d* (£1.27½) per month, from which their clothing, living costs and tobacco were deducted.

The seaman was a brave, exotic and rather feckless creature, as seen by a ship's surgeon:

> The mind, by custom and example, is thus trained to brave the fury of the elements in their different forms, with a degree of contempt at danger and death that is to be met nowhere else. Excluded by the employment which they have chosen from all society but people of similar dispositions, the

deficiencies of education are not felt, and information on general affairs is seldom courted. Their pride consists in being reputed a thorough bred seaman; and they look upon all landmen, as being of an inferior order . . . their money is lavished with the most thoughtless profusion; fine clothes for his girl, a silver watch, and silver buckles for himself, are often the sole return for years of labour and hardship. When his officer refuses him leave to go on shore, his purse is sometimes with the coldest indifference consigned to the deep, that it may no longer remind him of pleasures he cannot command.

Skilled seamen made up about 40 per cent of the crew in an average ship. Some of the others were craftsmen such as carpenters, coopers and skilled metalworkers. Others were servants. Up to a fifth of the men on board were marines, wearing the red coats of the army and commanded by officers and sergeants in typical military fashion. Some of the crew were boys under training, often recruited by bodies such as the Marine Society, which took poor boys from the streets and slums of the big cities, issued them with clothes and sent them to the navy.

Others were landsmen, often with no skills that were useful on board ship, and often they had the worst time of it. A few of them were ex-prisoners, but not nearly as many as popular legend suggests, for the navy did not like to take hardened criminals into its ranks. They might take smugglers who had good sailing skills, or debtors, or innocent men who needed the naval bounty to secure their release from jail. Some had recently been made unemployed in declining trades such as hand-loom weaving, some were lured into the navy by huge sums offered as bounty. This was especially true in 1795, when a law was passed requiring each local authority to send a specific number of men to the navy. Skilled seamen were preferred as always, and counted double on the final tally, but in desperation many landsmen were recruited by the offers of bounty of up to £70, five years wages for a seaman. On board ship, these men might learn to become sailors, but only those who started at the age of about 25 or less were likely to do so. The rest were doomed to spend many years in menial jobs.

CHAPTER 2

The Ship

A new recruit to the navy, whether willing or not, would probably find himself on board a small vessel known as a press tender to take him to the fleet. This was often a scene of horror. According to William Hay,

> Upon getting on board this vessel, we were ordered down in the hold, and the grating was put over us; as well as a guard of marines placed round the hatchway, with their muskets loaded and fixed bayonets, as though we had been culprits of the first degree, or capital convicts. In this place we spent the day and the following night huddled together, for there was not room to sit or stand separate.

After that the man might be taken to a depot ship at one of the great naval anchorages, the Nore in the mouth of the Thames, Spithead off Portsmouth, or Plymouth Sound. Then he would be assigned to a sea-going ship, which might be anything from a great three-decker of more than a hundred guns, to a tiny two-masted brig or schooner with ten or twelve 'pop-guns'.

The first thing anyone would notice on approaching a ship would be the great height of the masts and the yards which projected from them and carried sails. There was a great mass of rigging, the black standing rigging that supported the masts, and the buff-coloured running rigging that was used to manipulate the yards and sails. Practically all the ships of Nelson's navy were propelled by sail, except for a few small gunboats that used oars. All the large ships had three masts, which were square-rigged. That meant that the sails were fitted across the ship and hung from yards, and were roughly square in shape. Each ship had a bowsprit, which projected diagonally forward of the hull above the figurehead and was used to spread sails and brace the mast. They were best at sailing with the wind behind and coming from about 45 degrees over the stern (on the quarter) or from right angles to the ship on one side or the other (on the beam). They were less effective when the wind was ahead – they could tack (zigzag) into the wind, but they would make very little progress, and captains usually preferred to wait for suitable winds, or follow routes that guaranteed them, for example the favourable trade winds.

Ships at the time of Nelson's navy were made almost entirely of wood, and even most of the fastenings that held the hull together were wooden pegs, known as trenails. There were some iron bolts above the waterline, but they had to be made in a copper alloy in the lower part of the ship. The underwater part of the hull was covered in copper to keep out shipworm and deter weed, and iron bolts in that area would cause electrolysis and decay of the iron and copper. The main ironwork in a ship consisted of the guns, ranged down each side on one, two or three decks, and firing through gunports that opened in the sides.

The decks of each ship were laid as low as possible to keep the guns, and therefore the centre of gravity, low. This was most marked in smaller ships, but even in a 74-gun ship the height between decks was no more than 7ft. In practice it was much less than that, as the beams supporting the deck were perhaps 14in thick, so the real height was less than 6ft. It was even less in the orlop deck below, and any man above average height would be almost bent double as he moved about.

Ships were usually known by their number of guns, anything from ten to a hundred. They were also given rates. A first rate had a hundred guns or more, a third rate had seventy to eighty, a fifth rate had thirty to forty-six – it was nothing to do with the quality of the ship. They were also known by the number of decks.

The largest ships in the fleet were the great three-deckers, carrying ninety guns and upwards. They were poor at sailing, but made up for it with great gun power. The extra space was often used to carry an admiral and his staff – Nelson used HMS *Victory* at the Battle of Trafalgar while his second-in-command Cuthbert Collingwood was in the *Royal Sovereign*, which also had one hundred guns.

The 74-gun ship of the third rate was one of the most common types in the fleet. It had its guns on two decks and was considered a ship of the line, able to stand in the line of battle with other ships and face the largest that the enemy might put up against it. It was a highly successful type, with a battery of 32-pound guns, which were the heaviest that could be used in practice, and better speed than a three-decker. There were sixteen of them among the twenty-seven ships of the line in the British fleet at Trafalgar, and eighty-seven (out of a total of 175 ships of the line) in the navy as a whole at that time. They were slightly less popular with the crews – they did not offer the fame and style of a great flagship, or the glamour of a frigate. The smallest ships of the line carried sixty-four guns, but the heaviest of them were only 24-pounders and they were obsolete for the line of battle. It was said in 1795, 'There is no difference of opinion respecting 64-gun ships being struck out of the rates. It is a fact that our naval officers either pray or swear against being appointed to serve on board them.' This did not prevent Horatio Nelson, then a senior captain, being overjoyed when offered the command of the *Agamemnon* in 1793, after five long years on the beach. 'After cloud comes sunshine. The Admiralty so smile on me, that I really am as much surprised as when they frowned.'

Frigates carried only a single deck of guns, and the deck below, though just above the waterline, was unarmed. Their guns were light, mostly 18-pounders, though 24-pounder frigates were coming into use. The frigate could sail well in almost any weather. With the main fleet, it was used to scout ahead and to transmit signals from the flagship. It could carry messages, escort merchant ships, or attack enemy commerce. This was the most popular role, for it allowed the officers and men to gain prize money from captured enemy ships. Captain Francis Austen tried hard to get the command of one, but his administrative abilities made him too valuable as flag captain to an admiral, so he never became rich like his sister's creation Captain Wentworth. The frigate was also popular with crews. Its lower deck had no guns and so there was more room for the men to live and take their recreation. It was a sleek, well-proportioned ship, popular with the public and with artists.

It was commonly believed that French warships were superior to British ones, especially frigates, which were found to be faster. Naval officers were always pleased to be appointed to a captured French ship, but they were designed for fair-weather sailing and had weaker structures, so that they did not survive well in rough weather, for example off Brest.

Sloops were like miniature frigates, carrying ten to twenty guns. Some had three masts, like the larger warships, some had only two and were known as brigs. Smaller vessels were usually fore- and aft-rigged. The most important sails were attached to booms and gaffs behind the mast, and could be hauled in much tighter, so that the ship could sail closer to the wind. There were two-masted schooners, but the favourite British type was the single-masted cutter. This had been copied from vessels used by smugglers in the English Channel. It had a wide hull to allow it to sail with the wind on the beam, and a very tall mast carrying large sails.

On arriving on board a ship of the line, the new crew member would climb up the wooden steps on the side to arrive in the centre of the ship, known as the waist. He would step onto a deck filled with guns on each side, and hatches, capstans and other encumbrances down the middle. Aft, towards the stern of the ship, was a raised deck known as the quarterdeck, which was reserved for officers and for men who had to go there on duty. The quarterdeck held the steering wheel, and it was from there that the movement of the ship was controlled. In a ship of the line the captain lived in a cabin just aft of the wheel, and could be called to the deck quickly in an emergency. Above and behind it was the poop deck, forming a roof to the captain's cabin and carrying a few light guns of large calibre, known as carronades.

Going below, the seaman would find himself on the lower deck in a two-decker, the middle deck in a three-decker. Again there were rows of guns on either side, pointing out through the gunports and taking up much of the space. As well as a gun battery, the lower deck was where most of the crew lived. They would sling their hammocks there, and eat their meals at tables fitted between the guns on each side.

Going further down into the ship, the seaman would come to the orlop deck. This was used mainly for storage, with the thick anchor cables stowed there, and store rooms for spare parts for the hull, rigging and guns. Below that was the hold, where food, water, beer and spirits were kept in wooden casks.

The aftermost part of each deck was reserved for the officers, according to rank. The captain's cabin had large windows opening out over the stern, perhaps with an open gallery. There were quarter galleries projecting from each side. These were mainly used as toilets, but also allowed the captain to look at the set of the sails without leaving his cabin. The captain had several compartments, used as his bedroom, his dining room and perhaps his office. But even he had to share his accommodation with several guns, and the whole structure had to be cleared away if the ship went into battle. Below that, in a three-decker, the admiral had his cabin, similar to the captain's, but slightly larger. He too had stern and quarter galleries.

The after end of the upper deck in a two-decker, or the middle deck in a three-decker, contained the wardroom. This was where the officers directly below the captain lived – the lieutenants, the marine officers, the master, surgeon and purser. Each had a cabin of his own, perhaps one of those down the side of the wardroom itself, perhaps on one of the decks below. It too was often shared with a gun, and was just big enough for a cot to sleep in, a sea chest and perhaps a chair and desk. There was a long table down the centre of the wardroom, where the officers ate their meals and took their recreation. They too had quarter galleries and windows looking over the stern, though not the open galleries that some captains and admirals enjoyed.

In a frigate or a smaller ship, the captain lived in a cabin aft on the upper deck, as there was no poop deck. The other officers lived in the gunroom, which was aft on the lower deck and had no stern windows.

Below the wardroom of a ship of the line, aft on the lower deck, was the gunroom, where some of the junior officers lived. It was no use for hammocks as the area swept out by the tiller made it impossible to sling them. Below that, aft on the orlop deck and deep in the bowels of the ship, was the cockpit and midshipmen's berth. Natural light rarely penetrated there, and it could be a place of horror, used as an operating theatre by the surgeon during a battle. In more normal times, the 'young gentlemen' training to become officers lived a rather unruly life.

CHAPTER 3

The Officers

The new member of the crew would soon become acquainted with the officers, warrant officers and petty officers of his ship. If it was a flagship there would be an admiral on board. Often he was a remote figure who kept aloof from the crew, though he would be seen on the quarterdeck every day. Nelson was rather more approachable. In 1804, as he was blockading the French in Toulon, one of the seamen knocked him down accidentally with a hammock. As the seaman picked him up with great dexterity, Nelson said, 'Man, it was not your fault but my own. I ought to have known better than to stand in your way.' His friend Admiral Collingwood was known as the 'sailor's friend' and made a point of getting to know the men. When he saw a lieutenant addressing a man as 'You, sir!' he insisted in setting an example.

'Jenkins, what is that man's name in the weather rigging?'

'Dan Swain, your honour.' . . .

'Dan Swain.'

'Sir.'

'The after end of that ratling is too high; let it down a handsbreadth.'

'Aye, aye, Sir.'

Sir John Jervis, the Earl of St Vincent, was a far fiercer figure who enforced naval discipline very rigidly. He was at least as strict with the officers as with the crews, when he issued his standing orders. He 'observed a flippancy in the behaviour of officers when coming upon the *Victory*'s quarterdeck and sometimes in receiving orders from a superior officer' which was to cease. He criticised the 'vain and supercilious conduct of young and inexperienced officers' who thought they did not have to obey Admiralty instructions, and complained that they did not 'exert themselves with vigilance and activity to prevent drunkenness among the people'. When he was transferred from the Mediterranean to the Channel Fleet, the officers of the latter body were said to have toasted, 'May the discipline of the Mediterranean Fleet never be introduced into the Channel.'

The captain might be almost equally remote, though he too would be on deck at moments of danger or difficulty, and he would probably inspect the men and their quarters from time to time. The captain had almost absolute power over the ship, with the right to assess the pay rates of most of the men, and to flog them if they broke his rules. Often he would produce a detailed set of orders on how the ship was to be run, such as those of Captain Riou of the frigate *Amazon*, who was killed under Nelson at the Battle of

Copenhagen. He was 'an interesting and delightful character . . . His pensiveness of look and reserve in his manner made strangers regard him as cold and repulsive, but this impression was soon removed, and all who knew him loved him.' Captains varied greatly in character and each could set the tone of the ship. Thomas Cochrane, Earl of Dundonald, had a reputation for daring and was partly the model for Jack Aubrey in the Patrick O'Brian books. James Gambier was deeply religious and got the nicknames of 'dismal Jimmy' and 'preaching Jemmy'. His habits of punishing swearing and making sure that only married women came on board in harbour made him deeply unpopular.

The first lieutenant was the man who really ran the ship, allocating the men to watches and gun crews, and supervising them at work. According to Captain Riou,

> He ought to know everything, see everything and have to do with everything that is to be known,

> seen or done in the ship; and make the captain acquainted therewith, that he may know . . . He is to visit every part of the ship continually – forward, in the store rooms, tiers, etc – and endeavour to the utmost of his abilities to see that the standing orders contained in this book are complied with by every individual to whom they are addressed, and report to the captain accordingly.

He got no more pay than the other lieutenants and lived among them in the wardroom, but he did not keep watches so he was able to get a full night's sleep, except in an emergency. He was also likely to be promoted if the ship distinguished herself in action. Often, first lieutenants were men who had risen the hard way. John Quillam, first lieutenant of the *Victory* at Trafalgar, was a Manxman who probably joined a ship in 1791 to escape from trouble at home. He fought at the Battle of Camperdown in 1797 as a master's mate and was a lieutenant by 1798. He was one of many officers who had come up 'through the hawsehole', for it was not too difficult for a seaman with a reasonable amount of education to gain a commission. His promotion prospects were slower than those of men with good connections, which was an advantage to Nelson, who needed him to run his flagship.

A 74-gun ship, with a crew of about 600, usually had five lieutenants, a typical frigate had three or four. Apart from the first lieutenant, they took it in turns to be in charge of the watch, supervising the sailing of the ship, deciding when to take or set sails, and calling the captain if there was a major change in the weather, or the enemy was sighted. Each was also in charge of a division of perhaps a hundred seamen, to supervise their welfare and discipline. He would make sure that each man kept himself clean and had suitable clothing, he would take an interest in his private affairs and perhaps speak up for him if he got into trouble. Each lieutenant was entitled to a cabin of his own, and a seat at the wardroom table.

He would share the accommodation with the marine

officers. A 74-gun ship might have three of them, headed by a captain. Unlike the naval lieutenants, their training was very slight and they were appointed by the Board of Admiralty, provided they seemed suitable and had good references. Often their men were dispersed among the gun crews in action, and the officers had little to do. Thoroughly bored during a voyage to Barbados in 1815, Captain Robert Clarke of the 74-gun ship *Swiftsure* spent his time reading novels and hoping to replenish the wardroom stock of wine with a visit to Madeira, or from one of the ships in the convoy. He drilled his men occasionally: 'In the forenoon exercised the marines quartered at small arms, at firing with blank cartridges, and changing their position on the poop occasionally, in which they acquitted themselves very well', but he cursed 'that villain Downey', who published romantic poems about sea life.

The master had a warrant from the Navy Board rather than the King's Commission as borne by the lieutenants and marine officers, but he was one of the most important figures on board. He was usually a former merchant seaman, perhaps a mate pressed into the navy. He was responsible for the navigation of the ship in the broadest sense – fixing the position and choosing the course to a destination, but also in handling the ship in tight corners such as tacking, anchoring or coming alongside.

The ship's chief medical officer was a surgeon rather than a physician. This meant that he had a rather low status, for a physician was usually trained at university, a surgeon by apprenticeship. He was skilled at amputation and had a general medical knowledge, but in the days before anaesthetic it was impossible for him to carry out any kind of delicate operation. Leonard Gillespie served as surgeon of the sloop *Racehorse* off the east coast of England and Scotland in 1787–91 and was thoroughly disillusioned with the life by the end:

> I left her without regret, rather rejoicing that my military bondage and my narrow confinement

within a sloop's wretched gunroom had expired, and sincerely wishing that I might never more be necessitated to serve on board a ship of war, when alas, indolence, intemperance, spleen, envy etc too often infect the crew and spread unhappiness and discord.

But later, in 1803–5, Gillespie became the physician in charge of the health of Nelson's Mediterranean Fleet, and painted a far rosier picture:

> Between the hours of seven and two there is plenty of time for business, study, writing and exercise, which different occupations, together with that of occasionally visiting the hospital of the ship when required by the surgeon, I endeavour to vary in such a manner as to afford me sufficient employment.

Physicians and surgeons made an indispensable contribution to the health of the navy, particularly in eliminating scurvy by the insistence on eating fresh vegetables. But no one doubted that the seaman's profession was a dangerous one. Casualties in battle were relatively light over twenty years of war, and only 6,663 men were lost in that way according to one estimate. This was partly because the British had the 'habit of victory' and won most of the major battles. At Trafalgar the British had 449 killed out of a total of 1,690 casualties; the French and Spanish had nearly ten times as many killed as well as 2,545 wounded and about 7,000 taken prisoner.

Deaths from shipwreck or fire amounted to more than 13,000, twice as many as died in battle. But the greatest number of all was the 72,000 men (out of a fleet that never numbered more than 142,000) who died of disease or from small accidents such as a fall from the rigging. Diseases such as yellow fever could spread very quickly through a ship, and others such as typhus were often brought on board by pressed or quota men.

The purser was the main supply officer of the ship, but his position was highly ambiguous. He was paid less than his messmates such as the master and surgeon, because he was expected to make a profit on some of his transactions. This naturally encouraged the idea that pursers swindled the crew out of their provisions, and so they were often unpopular. Surgeon Leonard Gillespie had mixed feelings about Joseph Jones, purser of the sloop *Racehorse* after two years in a gunroom with him.

> Facetious, pleasant, humorous and somewhat worthy; conciliating in his address and ever well received, especially by the ladies; but unhappy in his mind, intemperate, fickle, weak-headed. In short a man dangerous not so much from his depravity as his weakness. I have had great reason to be thankful that I have steered clear of quarrelling with him . . .

Each ship was entitled to carry a chaplain. The post often went unfilled since the conditions of service were poor, though Nelson was a very religious man and nearly always carried one and tried to ensure that the ships under him did too. Edward Mangin served briefly as a chaplain in the 74-gun *Gloucester* in 1812, but soon began to question his role: 'nothing can possibly be more unsuitable or more awkwardly situated than a clergyman in a ship of war; every object around him is at variance with the sensibilities of a rational and enlightened mind'. His attempts to rebuke the seaman for 'profane swearing and intemperate language of every kind' were soon abandoned.

Nelson's Chaplain, Alexander John Scott, was a remarkable figure whose skills went far beyond his preaching. He was an expert linguist, an intelligence agent in Catalonia and Sardinia, an obsessive book collector and one of the admiral's chief advisers. He was odd in appearance, with a 'fine and intellectual' forehead, 'pale, thin and tall in person, very romantic and enthusiastic'.

If the chaplain was a benign figure, the boatswain was far more terrifying. He was one of the three 'standing officers', so called because they stayed with the ship even if she was taken out of service and 'laid up in ordinary'. Like his colleagues the gunner and the carpenter, he was largely responsible for maintenance, of the rigging in his case. He had a storeroom and kept accounts, with several boatswain's mates to assist him. But to the crew, he was best known as the ship's chief disciplinarian. He and his mates roused the crew from their hammocks in the morning, often with the cry 'show a leg' to find out if the occupants were men or women. They used rope's ends and canes to 'start' the crew, to encourage them to greater activity. The boatswain's mates wielded the cat-o'-nine-tails at floggings.

The gunner was a more intellectual figure, though like the boatswain he too was a warrant officer who had risen from the ranks. William Rivers, who was gunner of the *Victory* at the time of Trafalgar, had served some time as a midshipman and master's mate, but apparently preferred the more immediate promotion to gunner. He kept meticulous and usually well-written notebooks on the technicalities of his profession. William Richardson was a petty officer in the frigate *Prompte* and was slightly surprised to be ordered to take charge of the gunners' stores in 1795, with the promise of a warrant later. He remained an acting gunner until he had completed the four years necessary to undergo the oral examination. A gunner had several mates under him, and a quarter-gunner for every four guns in the ship. He had little to do with the firing of the guns, which was supervised by the commissioned officers, but he was in charge of the maintenance, and especially of the safe and careful stowage of the powder.

Unlike the other standing officers, the ship's carpenter had served an apprenticeship, often in the Royal Dockyards. He had more responsibility than his colleagues in the sense that he kept the ship afloat.

He had a crew of one mate and eight skilled men in a 74-gun ship, four in a frigate.

The standing officers each had their own cabins, usually on the orlop deck. Because of their permanent employment they were often allowed to keep their families on board. William Richardson, gunner of the captured Dutch 60-gun ship *Tromp*, reluctantly agreed to let his wife come on a trip to Madeira in 1799: 'so (after some entreaty) I gave my consent, especially as the captain's, the master's, the purser's, and boatswain's wives were going with them . . . a person would have thought they were insane wishing to go to such a sickly country'.

CHAPTER 4

Living on Board

In most ships the crew was divided into two watches, so that when the ship was at sea one group would be on duty while the other rested or slept. Some had three watches, so that only a third was on duty at once during the night. A watch lasted for 4 hours, except the two 2-hour dog watches between four and eight in the afternoon, which were intended to vary the routine from day to day. With the two-watch system a man would never have more than 4 hours continuously in his hammock while the ship was at sea, perhaps rather less as he was roused at least a quarter of an hour early for one watch, and took some time to get off duty and undress at the end of it.

All this was liable to interruption if the ship was called to action stations or an intricate manoeuvre had to be carried out. Work during the night watches was not particularly hard. Men were needed to steer the ship and act as lookouts, while the others might be called upon to trim the sails or reduce the amount carried if the weather looked like worsening. But for much of the time the men could generally relax. They might be allowed to play games or sing songs, and in some ships they were even allowed to sleep on deck.

During each watch, time was marked by the ringing of the ship's bell every half hour. Thus three bells meant an hour and a half into the watch, and eight bells meant 4 hours and the end of the watch.

Some men, such as the cook, coopers, writers (clerks) and servants worked mostly in the daytime. They kept no watch and were known to the rest of the crew as idlers. They too might be called out in an emergency, and everyone had a role to play if the ship entered battle.

At sea, the typical ship's day began early in the morning when the boatswain's mates roused the off-watch seamen from their hammocks with loud cries and often the use of canes. Hammocks were unlashed, rolled up in tight cylinders and stowed in racks round the upper decks. The decks were scrubbed while the cooks prepared breakfast, which was served around 7 a.m. After that both watches and the idlers were on duty for the forenoon watch between eight and twelve, perhaps carrying out exercises with the sails or drill with the guns, or doing maintenance work about the hull and rigging. At noon the officers went off to take a sight of the sun, vital for navigation purposes. Dinner was served soon afterwards. It was the crew's main meal, and often the happiest time of the day.

It was often the case that the sailor did not have the right to choose whether he was in the navy or not, or in which ship he was to serve. He did however have a good deal of choice of his messmates, the men he ate his meals and took his recreation with. A mess was a group of men, whose number varied from ship to ship. Often they had a table to themselves, between a pair of guns in a ship of the line, but it was not unknown for two messes to share the same table. Men were allowed to get together to form messes, and by tradition any man had the right to ask the first lieutenant to change the mess on the first day of each month. Men of similar backgrounds tended to congregate together – perhaps from the same town, or men who had sailed together before, or novices at the same state of nautical knowledge. A few social isolates had to take meals on their own. For any true seaman, the most important thing in the world was the respect of his messmates. Old salts would tell yarns together, and would relish their own fearlessness, and the courage of those around them. It was this kind of conversation that inspired the seaman to perform great feats of valour.

Preparations for the meal began in the middle of the morning. One man from the mess would be cook of the day. He would go to the orlop deck where the food would be issued to him by 'Jack in the dust', the purser's assistant. He might prepare it to some extent himself, then he would take it to the galley, which was situated forward on the upper deck, under the forecastle on a two-decker. The cook himself had very little culinary skill and was usually an old seaman who had lost at least one limb and was given the job in lieu of a pension. He and his assistants would simply boil the food given to them in a great kettle, which was part of the galley stove. The cooks of the messes would arrive just before dinner to collect the cooked food, perhaps some kind of stew. Half a pint of rum was issued to each man at the same time, and the meal began. Dinnertime was at least an hour long on most ships, perhaps an hour and a half. Both watches were allowed to eat together, though a few helmsmen and lookouts had to be left on duty. Captains were careful not to interrupt the meal except in the case of the most urgent necessity.

Officially, the men were allowed 2 pounds of beef on two days a week, and a pound of pork on two other days. Every day they were given a pound of biscuit, a kind of unleavened bread, and during the course of the week they had 1½ pints of oatmeal, 2 pints of pease, 6 pounds of sugar and the same amount of butter, and 12 ounces of cheese. They were allowed a gallon of beer per day, or the equivalent in spirits when beer was not available. Brandy and wine were issued on the Mediterranean station, rum mainly in the West Indies, for it was not yet established as the main naval drink. The diet was adequate in terms of nourishment, but there was nothing in it to prevent scurvy, and by Nelson's time pursers were supplementing it by 'portable' or condensed soup, sauerkraut, lemon juice and the well-known (but far less effective) lime juice. In foreign waters the men were often fed with local supplies.

After dinner, one watch was on duty while the other rested. At four in the afternoon they had supper, which was not unlike dinner and with another issue of rum but usually on a smaller scale. The ship went into the dog watches, then at eight 'the watch was set'. The captain would retire to his cabin, the men would take the hammocks and set them up below, and the watch on duty took over the ship under one of the lieutenants. This watch was relieved at midnight, and the final change took place at 4 a.m., after which it was almost time to begin the ship's day again.

Officers slept in small canvas beds known as cots, while each seaman had two hammocks of his own, so that one could be washed while the other was in use. Each was made of canvas with a series of ropes known as knittles at each end. It was slung from the beams of the deck above, and it was at night-time that the ship seemed most crowded. Men were allocated places or berths by the first lieutenant, usually arranged with the watches alternating. The standard allowance was 14in per man, though that was mitigated if one watch was on deck. Petty officers were allowed more space and had berths close to the sides of the ship, giving a certain amount of privacy. The hammock itself was only a receptacle for a bed, for it contained a flock mattress, pillow and blankets. Seamen claimed that the hammock was comfortable in a moving ship, though officers were not keen to give up their cots and return to the hammocks they had used as midshipmen.

Officers wore uniforms with dark blue jackets (though not as dark as modern navy blue). Commissioned officers had full dress uniforms for formal occasions, and 'undress' for everyday wear. Captains and admirals had a good deal of gold braid on their sleeves, and after 1795 they wore gold epaulettes. For lieutenants, the main colour was white, large white lapels in full dress, and white trim on undress. A midshipman wore a white collar patch (as he still does today) and warrant officers had plain blue uniforms. White knee breeches with stockings were worn most of the time, and at Trafalgar Nelson advised one of his lieutenants not to wear boots, as they would be difficult to remove if he were wounded. There were no regulations about headgear, but most preferred the cocked hat, which could be removed easily to salute a superior.

There was no uniform for the lower deck, but seamen had a very distinctive style of their own – if they were ashore and wearing the 'long clothes' of a landsman, they were very conscious of being in disguise against the press gang. The broad seaman's collar with three white stripes was still well in the future, but the seaman preferred wide trousers and short jackets, contrasting with the landsman's long tailcoat and breeches. Of course clothes would wear out on a long voyage, and men recruited under the Quota Acts, for example, often came on board in rags or with very unsuitable clothing. They might buy a certain amount from 'bumboats' that came alongside in port, but the main supply was from the ship's purser. They were allowed to buy 'slops' out of their wages, so a certain amount of uniformity began to set in. Though the clothes were the man's own property, many captains laid down a minimum amount that each man had to have. For Captain Riou in the *Amazon*, this consisted of two blue jackets, three striped Guernsey waistcoats, three pairs of white duck trousers and two in blue, two loose shirts or banyans, one pair of drawers, four striped shirts, two black silk handkerchiefs, three pairs of stockings, two pairs of shoes and two round hats with small brims. But most seamen took a good deal of pride in their dress, and Riou was equally anxious that they should not go to extremes: 'Flimsy white trousers, cloth waistcoats of variegated colours and other trash are only brought on board to catch the eye of and cheat the inexperienced boys.'

The men were expected to wash their clothes twice a week, and certain days were set aside for drying them on the rigging. They could also make their own, and most seamen were skilled with needle and thread.

Traditionally, each Wednesday afternoon was set aside as a 'make and mend' day to allow them to do this.

In their spare time, the men devised their own entertainments. The more experienced of them loved telling yarns, though the same ones must have been repeated many times over on a long voyage. Some were involved in handicrafts such as modelling or embroidery. Singing was always popular, though not the shanties, or work songs, associated with the merchant service: seamen loved romantic songs like 'Ladies of Spain', or dirges. A visitor on HMS *Gibraltar* wrote in 1811:

> It is ridiculous to hear the sailors lie and sing in their hammocks of an evening. They chant the most dismal ditties in the world and the words be ever so merry, yet the tune is one and the same, namely 'Admiral Hosier's Ghost'.

Fiddling was equally popular, and most captains made sure that they had at least one player on board. The visitor to the *Gibraltar* wrote:

> They never seemed to dance with any spirit unless they had an old black to fiddle to them, of the name of Bond. He was a most curious fellow and cannot play on his instrument unless it be accompanied by his voice, or rather his throat, which makes a rumbling noise, growing louder and louder the longer he fiddles, so that at last his own sounds are much stronger than those of his catgut.

Men had very limited shore leave because of the fear of desertion, but were allowed to send letters home at a cheap rate. Literate seamen could get extra money or alcohol by writing for their colleagues, and reading out the replies. Ships of the line often spent a good deal of time in port in anchorages such as Spithead off Portsmouth, and in that case women were allowed on board. In theory they were the wives of the men, but only a religious zealot like Captain Gambier would try to enforce that rule, and often large numbers of prostitutes arrived, perhaps to stay on

board for several days in very crowded and insanitary conditions.

Naval discipline was very different from that of the army, and sailors regarded themselves as far superior to soldiers or marines. One captain wrote:

> The character of the seaman is one which is inimical to any form or parade, while in the soldier precision of movement and an approach to mechanism form the very essence of his utility. This thoughtlessness, this unrestrained dash in the execution of a seaman's duty it would be well to encourage . . . But all attempt to drill the seaman into unnecessary military parade will tend to break down the whole of his natural character . . .

The most they would do was to 'toe the line' – to stand along the line or seam where two of the deck planks joined. Instead, they had a different kind of discipline, based on the need for teamwork when working in the rigging, hauling on ropes or working guns. Boatswains' mates might stand by with cane 'starters' to hit any man they thought to be slacking, but in a well-run ship that was not necessary, and many officers banned it. In 1809 Captain Corbett of the frigate *Neriede* was court-martialled for brutality, but only found guilty of issuing his petty officers with 'sticks of an improper size, and such as are not usual in His Majesty's Service'.

For serious offences, a man might be brought before the captain, who had the legal right to sentence him to up to a dozen lashes for each offence (but he often ordered more than that). If he was found guilty, the crew was assembled on deck, and often the marines were drawn up above them on the quarterdeck with muskets and fixed bayonets. He was stripped to the waist and lashed to a grating against the ship's side. The boatswain's mate wielded the cat-o'-nine-tails, made up of nine strands of rope. Many men were never flogged in their entire naval career;

some could not avoid it. Patrick Purcell of HMS *Blake*, for example, was flogged eight times from 1809 to 1812. The ship was run quite harshly by Edward Codrington, with 144 floggings in fourteen months. This contrasted with the optimistic view of the visitor to HMS *Gibraltar*, who commented, 'Not one in 200, out of 600 or 700 men, ever allow themselves to be thus disgraced.'

An officer who committed an offence would usually be sent before a court martial, composed of at least five captains. A seaman accused of a serious crime would also face a court martial, and then the stakes were much higher. The court had the right to order the death penalty for many crimes, including mutiny and assisting the enemy as well as the more usual ones of murder and some forms of theft – in many respects this reflected civil society, where death by hanging was quite normal for comparatively trivial crimes. The court could also award the man an unlimited amount of lashes with the cat, often for desertion. This sentence was known as flogging round the fleet and was the cruellest of the day. The man was lashed up in a ship's launch and rowed from one ship to another, to receive twenty-five lashes opposite each until a surgeon ordered the punishment suspended for the moment.

Mutiny was the most serious offence as far as naval officers were concerned, but it was quite common. It came in three different levels. At the top was a kind of naval revolution in which the officers were overthrown and either killed or cast adrift, as happened with Captain Bligh of the *Bounty* in 1789. The most serious outbreak of this kind was in the frigate *Hermione* in 1797, when Captain Pigot ordered the last men of the yardarm to be flogged, and two fell to their deaths. The crew revolted and took the ship into a Spanish West Indian port. She was recaptured in a famous 'cutting out' action by HMS *Surprise*, and the Admiralty spared no effort to track down the ringleaders over the years.

A more moderate form of mutiny was a kind of naval strike, in which a whole crew, or even a whole fleet, refused to sail or perform a task unless certain conditions were met. This was quite common if certain rules were broken, for example if a crew was sent on foreign service without being paid first, though this sort of mutiny rarely happened at sea. In 1779, however, the men of the *Prince George* refused to bring their hammocks on deck for airing. The Captain, Phillip Patton, called them on deck, explained why it was necessary, and then ordered individual men and small parties until they complied. Mutinies like this rarely reached even the ship's log book, but they took place on a far larger scale in the anchorages at Spithead and the Nore in 1797, when whole fleets revolted against poor pay and conditions. In the first case concessions were made and the navy had its first pay rise for nearly a century and a half. At the Nore, the demands were far more difficult to meet and eventually the revolt was put down. Many men, including the ringleader Richard Parker, were hanged.

The third and most common kind of mutiny was on a far smaller scale, when one or more men refused to obey orders. This happened, for example, in 1798 when the men of the *Mars* were refused permission to have women on board and Thomas Perkins shouted out, 'Come on, you men, what do you say? Let's all go on shore after the women. I will be the first to make a break.' He earned a court martial and a flogging, but there were far more cases that were dealt with on board ship.

The sea life had many dangers: more than 13,000 men were lost through shipwreck and fire between 1793 and 1815. Eighteen ships of the line, three 50-gun ships, forty-three frigates and sixty-two sloops and smaller vessels were lost by accident between 1783 and 1815 alone. Fire in a wooden ship was the most fearsome thing, and Admiral Keith was lucky to be ashore when his flagship, the 100-gun *Queen Charlotte*, was burned to the waterline in 1800 with the loss of 673 men, four-fifths of her crew.

Shipwreck was almost as serious, and John Wetherell describes the loss of the frigate *Hussar* on the Saintes rocks off the coast of France in 1804:

The ship fell over on her starboard beam ends. Then knock off pumping and get the topmasts over the side to prevent her falling any farther over. This was a scene of confusion, some were crying out for the lord to help them, others contriving to raise some grog, some packing up their cloaths, others hopeing she Never would float again, &c, &c. We fired Minuite guns, hove up rockets for help, but all to no avail . . .

CHAPTER 5

Sailing the Ship

A sailor had to master many skills. He could tie many different kinds of knot, from the simple and well-known reef knot and bowline, to the Matthew Walker and the single diamond knot. He could work with ropes in various ways, forming decorative Turk's heads in the ends of some, or worming, parcelling and serving the shrouds which supported the masts. On orders to tack ship or take in sail, he had to be able to find the right rope in the dark or when drunk from rum, and haul on it to order. He was expected to climb up 100ft of mast in a storm or a rough sea to set or take in sail, or to work aloft 4 hours at a time on maintenance work or as a lookout. A fully skilled man, rated as an able seaman, could steer the ship, help the sailmaker to repair the canvas, or cast the lead to find the depth of water under the ship. Yet the seaman had not usually served an apprenticeship, was not a member of a guild and was not regarded as a skilled artisan like say a cooper or a carpenter. This was rather unfair, as every seaman had a great deal to learn.

In fact, seamanship was rather like a language. It was not too difficult to learn provided one was brought up in the right environment at the right age, but it was almost impossible to become fluent if too old, or trained by artificial means. In any case, it was not just the skill that made a true seaman, but his ability to withstand hardship and danger. In a common phrase at the time, a man had to be 'bred to the sea'. As a result, in another common phrase, he would become 'inured to the hardship of a sea life'.

An experienced seaman was adept at working in the rigging, while a young man might adopt a carefree attitude, as described by Captain Marryat:

> I had become from habit extremely active, and so fond of displaying my newly acquired gymnastics, called by the sailors 'sky-larking', that my speedy exit was often prognosticated by the old quarter-masters, and even by the officers. It was clearly understood that I was either to be drowned or was to break my neck; for the latter I took my chance pretty fairly, going up and down the rigging like a monkey. Few of the topmen could equal me in speed, still fewer surpass me in feats of daring activity. I could run along the topsail yards out to the yard-arm, or go from one mast to the other by the stays, or down on the deck in the twinkling of an eye by the topsail halyards . . .

Sailors, especially the less skilled men, also had to do a good deal of hard labour – pulling on ropes, pushing on capstan bars, and cleaning the decks.

There were also a number of women on board many warships even at sea, despite this being forbidden by Admiralty regulation. It is possible that up to a hundred women were on board the 74-gun *Goliath* at the Battle of the Nile, for example, with a crew of 650 men. They found work as nurses and cooks, though their role is largely hidden from history. They became less common in later years as regulations were enforced more rigidly, and probably far fewer were at Trafalgar.

For working the ship, the seamen of each watch were divided into six main groups, according to skills. There were three groups of topmen, one for each mast. They were usually young men at the peak of their careers, fully grown and highly skilled but energetic enough to work hard and at great speed. Often the mizzen mast, the smallest, had a few boys attached for training. Each group was headed by a petty officer, the captain of the top. On the decks below, the men of the forecastle division were older but also quite experienced, for they had to do skilled work in raising the anchor. The men in the quarterdeck were less skilled, though they were usually presentable in appearance and manners as they had to work close to the officers. Between the forecastle and the quarter-deck was where the waisters worked, the least skilled group, good only for scrubbing decks and hauling on ropes.

Though every seaman was immensely proud of his own skill, it was teamwork that made the ship work. Warships of the day rarely came alongside a pier or a jetty, except when going into a dockyard for major repairs, so most voyages began with the raising of the anchor. The heavy work was done by seamen and marines pushing at the bars of the capstan, up to 200 men at a time. The anchor cable was made of very thick rope, up to 8in in diameter, and it was too large to go round the capstan. Instead, an endless rope called the messenger was used. This was attached to each part of the cable as it came up by light ropes known as nippers, and the name was eventually transferred to the ship's boys who held them and walked back with the cable towards the capstan. One party worked below in the orlop deck stowing the cable in tiers, while more skilled men stood on the forecastle. As soon as the ring of the anchor broke surface, it was attached to a hook dangling from the cathead, a small wooden crane projecting from the bow. The anchor was hoisted out of the water with its stock vertical, then its lower end, the crown, was raised to 'fish' the anchor, to stow it in a safe position against the ship's side, where its metal flukes would not do too much damage by bashing into the wooden planks.

Meanwhile another party was working aloft to loose the sails. Men would go out along the yards with their feet on the footropes, and their bodies resting against the yard itself. When the time came they untied the gaskets, ropes that held the sail tight to the yard. Others on deck would pull on the ropes to set the sail – the sheets which extended the corners, and the braces which set the angle of the sail to the wind. As the ship began to gather speed, more sails would be set according to the wind conditions. The topsails were usually set first. Below them were the lower sails, the courses, which came down almost to the level of the deck. If the wind was light, then the upper sails on each mast – the topgallants and the royals – would also be set. If they were trying to sail close to the wind, then the fore and aft sails were set. These consisted of staysails set on the stays between the masts; the triangular jibs set from the stays between the foremast and the bowsprit which projected ahead of the ship; and the quadrilateral mizzen course, which was fitted aft of the mast, with a wooden gaff supporting it from above and a boom from below.

Once clear of the anchorage, the officer of the watch would take charge of the sailing. He would decide when to set more sail or take some in (though he might have instructions to call the captain if the wind got very strong). Some sails, such as the topsails, could be reefed down, with their area reduced to a minimum in strong winds. Tackles were placed to haul on ropes attached some way up each side of the sail, and along the sail were light ropes known as reef points. The topmen would go aloft to tie these together across the yard.

For good sailing, the officers preferred to have the wind coming over one side of the ship or the other – a reach. Each yard would be braced round to the appropriate angle, about 15 degrees to the wind, and it would act rather like an aeroplane wing, though in the vertical rather than the horizontal plane. Sailing was slightly less effective if the wind was from directly behind, as one sail would tend to mask another. If sailing close to the wind, each yard would be braced round as far as possible, but at best the ship could only sail about one point, or 22½ degrees, into the wind – compared with two points, or 45 degrees, for a modern yacht. Even then, the ship was almost certainly being pushed sideways by the wind, so she would make little progress. Captains usually preferred to wait for a favourable wind or tide, and chose routes where they were likely to find them. Even so, it was generally impossible to predict when a sailing ship would arrive at her destination.

Sailing into the wind was known as beating to windward. The ship would be steered on a zigzag course, and turned to bring the wind on the other side. If she was turned by bringing the bows into the wind, this was known as tacking, but it required careful coordination of the movements of the sails, and was not always possible with an inexperienced crew or in rough seas. In that case the ship would be turned by wearing, turning her stern to the wind. It was easier to do, but took longer and lost a certain amount of ground. Often the whole crew was needed on deck for tacking or wearing, as all the yards had to be shifted at exactly the right moment. On long voyages, tacking or wearing at night would often be timed for the change-over of the watches so that men were not roused